Contents

Foreword   4

Early Policing and the Constabulary of Ireland   5

The Royal Irish Constabulary   16

The Ulster Special Constabulary   33

The Royal Ulster Constabulary   45

The Police Service of Northern Ireland   75

Other Antecedent and Related Forces: 89

    Londonderry Borough Police (1849 to 1870)   89

    Belfast Town Police   91

    Irish Revenue Police   92

    The Dublin Metropolitan Police   92

    Belfast Harbour Police   94

Authors' Biographies   96

Foreword

Policing in Ireland has always been challenging. From the days of Sir Robert Peel's original Peace Preservation Force, of the early 1800s, through to today's Police Service of Northern Ireland, each generation of officers have had different but often strangely similar difficulties and challenges to face.

This book sets out to illustrate and enlighten readers about a policing history distinct from the rest of the UK, one in which officers have often had to deal with threats to life and limb on a scale and regularity unknown elsewhere.

The images contained within are mainly drawn from the collection held by The Police Museum in Belfast and reflect the contrast between civil and security based policing, which has defined the history of policing here.

I would like to convey my thanks to David Orr, a publisher of several police and military histories in his own right, and Hugh Forrester, Curator of the Police Museum, for their work in bringing this volume together. I regard it as a worthy tribute to all the officers who down the years have given their service, and often unfortunately their lives, in serving and protecting their community.

J. A. Harris
Deputy Chief Constable
Chair, Police Historical Society (NI)

Early Policing and the Constabulary of Ireland

Ireland at the end of the eighteenth century was in a state of political and social turmoil, culminating in the 1798 Rebellion and Act of Union of 1801. The period saw the appearance of many secret societies in rural areas aimed at opposing increasing Anglicisation of what were perceived as traditional patterns of landholding and tenantry. Such societies were secret, oath-bound, and carried out acts of arbitrary violence against individuals, their property and animals, leading to the uniquely Irish offence of the 'outrage.' The existing magistracy became increasingly unable to deal with this rural crime, which led to law and order being in a state of paralysis – if not breakdown – in many areas.

Against this background, the history of organised policing in Ireland can be said to begin with the Act of 1787 to establish Baronial Constables throughout Ireland. These were appointed by local magistrates and carried out only minor policing duties, such as searching for stolen goods. Any major law and order disturbances were handled by the army or locally recruited militia or yeomanry.

The old 'Barnies' (as they came to be called) proved relatively ineffective due to their age and lack of training and were subject to only loose control by local magistrates. The increasing disorder in many counties due to the activities of secret societies – often called 'Ribbonmen', 'Whiteboys', 'Peep-o-Day Boys ' etc. – led the British administration based in Dublin to consider alternative solutions to the policing problem.

Robert Peel, when Chief Secretary for Ireland, was confronted with the crisis in law and order and after unsuccessful attempts at reforming the Irish bench, introduced the innovation of a centralised police force with the Peace Preservation Act of 1814. Under this, an area proclaimed to be in a state of disturbance could have a force of mounted police raised by the government and sent into it under a Chief Constable, who was also a stipendiary magistrate. The activities of these forces was aimed solely at countering the activities of the secret societies and was seen as a purely temporary measure, as the force could be withdrawn and disbanded after an area was declared pacified. A punitive measure lay in the fact that the cost of raising and paying for the force was directly transferred to the county ratepayers to pay for the 'luxury of their disturbance'.

The Peace Preservation Force was introduced and was recruited chiefly from army ex-cavalry non-commissioned officers (NCOs). As they wore no uniform, many continued to wear their old cavalry tunics, which is reputed to be the reason why Sergeant's-rank chevrons in subsequent forces and into the Police Service of Northern Ireland (PSNI) are worn on the lower cuff, rather than the upper arm.

Soon after their first appearance, members of the force acquired the nickname of 'Peelers' which has persisted to the present day; in contrast to England where the nickname of 'Bobbies' was used instead.

The next development was the introduction from 1822 of organised police forces for the whole of Ireland, organised on a county basis. Local magistrates were allowed a wide degree of appointment and control over the police, which soon led to accusations of corruption and manipulation that led to their amalgamation into a single centralised force – the Constabulary of Ireland – in 1836.

The Constabulary of Ireland heralded a new start in policing for Ireland as it comprised a single unified force, controlled centrally by the British administration in Dublin with no local involvement or influences, which had compromised earlier policing. It was an armed semi-military barracked force operating under strict discipline and had more in common with the *gendarmeries* of continental Europe than the local police forces being set up in England at the time.

An organisational and rank system unique to Ireland was adopted with an Inspector General based in Dublin, under which there was a system of counties under County Inspectors, districts under Sub – and later District – Inspectors, and larger stations under Head Constables, Constables, and Sub Constables (the use of military ranks was eschewed and the rank of Sergeant was not adopted until 1883).

Policemen were prohibited from joining any political or religious organisations (excluding the Society of Freemasons) and were not allowed to serve in their native or wife's native areas, aimed at ensuring their impartiality.

The force had its own Code of Regulations in 1837 and training centre from 1842 at Phoenix Park in Dublin, at which every recruit received six months' training on appointment. Copying the light infantry of the British army, the Constabulary adopted rifle green as its uniform colour; the concept of which persists until today. Many other features of the light infantry were adopted that persisted into the RUC, such as the adoption of a quick marching step and the carrying of carbines at the trail.

A cadet system of entry was introduced whereby suitably qualified young gentlemen could upon examination enter the Constabulary and after training be appointed to rank of Inspector. This system, which mirrored officer entry into the British army, continued into the Royal Ulster Constabulary (RUC) until after the Second World War.

In addition to its policing duties the Constabulary from the 1840s carried out a range of other duties, as often the only representatives of central government in local areas. These included fire-fighting, census taking, acting as Inspectors of Weights and Measures, and the collection of agricultural statistics, among others. Illicit distillation was widespread in many rural areas and the Constabulary in concert with the Irish Revenue Police worked to combat this. Their success was such that the Revenue Police were disbanded in 1857, and the duty passed solely to the Constabulary.

Extreme violence was often shown to the early Constabulary as they were seen as agents of unpopular government policies, such as during the 'Tithe War' of the 1830s. The force was seen by many in government as a force for moral good in Ireland, due to their strict discipline, military smartness, and bearing. The new force started to attract many recruits due to the fact that it was one of the few careers in nineteenth-century Ireland which offered secure pensionable employment, and most recruits came from a rural faming background; the rigours of which were seen as being best-suited to constabulary life.

The advantage of having an armed, centrally controlled police was evident to the government, as the danger of an armed nationalist insurrection – such as the Great Rebellion of 1798 – was a constant concern. The Constabulary, with superior numbers, firepower and nationwide local knowledge, was able to thwart several armed uprisings, such as that of Young Ireland in 1848 and, more significantly, the Fenian Rising of 1867.

Officer's silver button of Lisburn and K. Day Constables *c*. 1760.
The Lisburn and Killutagh Day Constables appear to have been a local watch force operating in the Lisburn area in the eighteenth century when the town was prospering under the brown linen industry.

Percussion horse pistols, 1829.
Presentation horse pistols engraved: 'From the Constabulary quartered in Garvagh District to their late esteemed and respected commander John L. Griffin, Esq, 12 July 1829, County Derry.'

J. L. Griffin was appointed to the Constabulary in 1825 as a Chief Constable and later Sub Inspector in Derry, Down, and Sligo, where he died in service in 1847.

These would have been carried in holsters on either side of an officer's saddle.

THE ILLUSTRATED LONDON NEWS

Obituary of Sir Robert Peel in
Illustrated London News, 1850.
Note the two policemen commemorating
his establishment of the Irish
Constabulary and London Metropolitan
Police.

Left: Silver snuffbox presented to Sir Richard Willcocks by the Chief Constables of the Limerick Constabulary, 1828.
Willcocks was Provincial Inspector General of the Munster Constabulary from 1822 to 1827.

Right: Constabulary of Ireland, 1838.
First uniforms worn by the all-Ireland force. 'Bell-topped' shakoes and a peaked forage cap are worn. Note also the brass shoulder scales worn. The mounted Sub Constable has cap lines on his shako and a pair of pistol holsters carried on his saddle. No badges are worn on caps; the only badge, a shamrock, was worn on the belt buckle plate.

Left: Officers at Phoenix Park Depot, Dublin, 1846.

A Chief Constable (later Sub/District Inspector) on left wearing full dress uniform for formal duties. He wears the 'Albert pot' shako. The officer on the right wears the undress uniform with the 'cheese cutter' forage cap.

The squad of men in the background are drilling with rifles and packs. Officers carried swords on formal duties until 1970 and recruits trained and 'passed-out' carrying rifles until the same date.

Right: Constabulary of Ireland, officer's full-dress uniform *c.* 1850.

Officers' tunics.

Irish Revenue Police undress tunic *c.* 1850 on left and Constabulary of Ireland officer's mess jacket, pre-1867, on right.

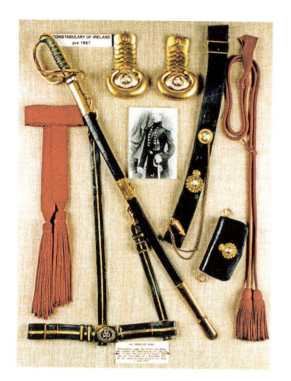

Left: Constabulary of Ireland officer's sword and appointments, pre-1867.

Right: Sub Inspector Henry Denny *c.* 1855.
Note the 'Albert pot' shako and large brass shoulder scales.

£10 REWARD.

I HEREBY OFFER A REWARD OF

TEN POUNDS

To any Person who shall, within Six Months from the date hereof, give such information as shall lead to the discovery and prosecution to conviction of the Person or Persons who, on the night of the 6th instant, went on the lands of *Tullogh*, in the Co. of *Tyrone*, and houghed a Cow, the property of *Thomas Blair*, of *Cookstown*.

J. H. RIDGE,

Sub-Inspector.

Cookstown, 11*th June*, 1844.

33,749—G.

'Outrage' reward notice, 1844.
Rural crimes or 'outrages' were common in the first half of the nineteenth century as a way for disgruntled groups to attack farmers and landowners.

'Houghing' was a form of cattle maiming in which the back hamstrings of a cow would be cut, usually under cover of darkness, so that the animal would have to be destroyed.

£40 REWARD.

WHEREAS, on the night of the 20th ult., a Rockite Notice was found fastened to a Tree near the Dwelling of *Alexander Hamilton*, at *Augherlarge*, in the Barony of *Dungannon*, County *Tyrone*, threatening his life should he not lower the Rents on the property of Mr. *Clavish:*

I HEREBY OFFER A REWARD OF

FORTY POUNDS

To any Person who shall, within Six Months from the date hereof, give such information as shall lead to the Arrest of the Person or Persons concerned in writing or posting said Notice. Payable on conviction.

J. H. RIDGE,

Sub-Inspector.

Cookstown, 9th November, 1849.

27977

'Rockite' reward notice, 1844.

'Rockites' was a name given to some of the secret factions who targeted landowners in rural Ireland. Notices such as these would be posted on trees or fences threatening landowners unless they lowered rents for their tenants.

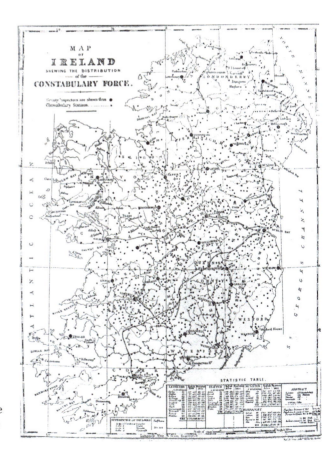

Map of Ireland showing location of constabulary barracks in 1852.

From *A Fortnight in Ireland* by Sir Francis Head. Larger dots represent headquarters; note the concentration of barracks in the south and centre.

THE MOUNTED STAFF CORPS

Left: Constabulary of Ireland cast-iron station badge, pre-1867.

Right: Members of The Mounted Staff Corps, 1855.
The Mounted Staff Corps were recruited from the Irish Constabulary to provide protection for the transport of supplies during the Crimean War.

Constabulary at Belfast, 1858.
The earliest known photograph of a Constabulary party shows officers and men in Belfast. Note the officers seated in the foreground in civilian clothes (only officers were permitted to wear civilian clothes when off duty).

The officer seated on the far right wears the full-dress uniform with shako, cross belt, and sword. The influence of the British light infantry uniform model can be seen here.

Other ranks – Constable and sub Constables – can be seen standing at the rear.

Note the stacked rifle carbines in the foreground, which were standard issue to other ranks.

Constabulary of Ireland single-shot percussion pistol, 1848.
Several hundred of these pistols were ordered from the Tower of London and issued to the first plain-clothes men.

Officer's pouch belt plate *c.* 1860.
The plate is in gilt with a silver harp; the crown is of the 'Guelphic' type used from the late 1850s.

Left: Constabulary headwear, 1822–1867.
Shown are the 'bell-top' shako (1822–40), the 'Albert' shako (1840s–1850s) and the 'Rifle' shako (1850s–1867).

The 'bell-top' shako was worn without badges and sealed in oilcloth against inclement weather.

Right: Sub Inspector George Hill Wray, 1864.
Wray had originally joined the Irish Revenue Police and was Sub Inspector at Ballynahinch in Co Down.

Constabulary Badge of Merit with one chevron.
Awarded to Sub Constable Patrick Hogan. The badge was worn on a leather strap on the left cuff.

Above:
Constabulary party beating off an attack on their barracks during the Fenian Rising, 1867. (From *Illustrated London News*)

Right:
Constabulary Medal (Ireland). Awarded to Sub Constable William Duggan, Glenbeigh, Co Kerry, for heroism during the Fenian Rising of 1867.

The Royal Irish Constabulary

The Fenian Rising of 1867 was the most serious attempt during the nineteenth century to overthrow British rule in Ireland. Organised from the United States, the Fenian Brotherhood aimed by armed insurrection to bring about an Irish socialist republic. However, their revolt focused on attacks on isolated police barracks, which were easily overcome by the Constabulary without the need for military aid. In recognition of the force's gallantry, Queen Victoria granted the title 'Royal' to the Constabulary and granted the used of the harp and crown belt device from the Illustrious Order of St Patrick to be used as the police badge.

The police had now become a constant in Irish life, with a barracks in every locality and its members being largely accepted and respected by local communities. The local Sergeant became as respected a local figure as the priest or solicitor and in an age of widespread illiteracy, people would come to the barracks for letters to be written or read. Policemen became regarded as desirable in the marriage market and many men married women from their posted areas.

However, the strict discipline, long hours and low pay led to widespread breaches in discipline, especially related to drinking or 'tippling.' Contemporary discipline sheets record most punishments, dis-ratings and dismissals being due to alcohol misuse.

By 1900 there was a network of over 1,500 barracks covering the length and breadth of the island and the strength of the force stood at around 10,000. The force well mirrored Irish society in terms of religion with over 80 per cent of the rank and file being Catholic, whereas the officer class – being largely Anglo-Irish – was predominantly Anglican.

The RIC was responsible for all policing with the exception of Dublin, which had its own city force, The Dublin Metropolitan Police (DMP), unarmed and modelled on the London Metropolitan Police. Belfast and Londonderry originally had their own locally controlled police forces, but due to their small size and ineffectiveness were disbanded and the job of policing transferred to the Constabulary.

Although the rural disorders which characterised the first half of the nineteenth century had largely subsided, tensions with local communities remained. These usually flared at election times and, in the north, during Orange and Green demonstrations, and in particular when the police had to carry out eviction duties.

Evictions on the large landed estates became known to the police as the 'most unpopular duty' due to the violence and animosity they aroused. Most police, being the sons of tenant farmers, felt some degree of sympathy with those being evicted, but were often seen by the public as active participants, rather than as merely protectors of the bailiffs' eviction parties. This reached a climax during the Land War of 1879–82, when the activities of the Land League in agitating to improve tenants' rights by actively opposing evictions and attacking landowners and their agents stretched the RIC to its limit.

Another difficult task for the RIC was the policing of Belfast, which had grown vastly in size during the nineteenth century due to the expansion the linen and other industries. Many of the new urban working-class population came from rural areas and brought sectarian or 'party' feelings with them. 'Flashpoint' areas emerged where working-class communities from either side of the religious divide met and often erupted into sustained rioting. Belfast suffered extreme rioting from the 1850s, which increased in intensity after Home Rule became an issue in the 1880s. Policing Belfast became the toughest policing job in the RIC and the major riots of 1886 and 1898 left many officers injured.

The mixture of normal policing and semi-military duties was unique to the RIC and this type of 'colonial' policing came to be seen as a model for other police forces throughout the British Empire. Many British colonial forces were set up on RIC lines – most famously the North West Mounted Police, later The Royal Canadian Mounted Police. British colonial officers from Africa and India came to train with the RIC in Dublin, much to the chagrin of nationalist journalists and politicians who unfavourably contrasted the friendly village 'Bobby' of England with the heavily armed *gendarme* of Ireland.

The period from the end of the Land War in the 1880s until the outbreak of the First World War was one of relative calm for the RIC. The land question, which gave rise to many disputes, receded and, apart from the stresses of dealing with periodic rioting in the north and the policing of the Belfast transport strike of 1907, the RIC confined itself to routine civil duties.

This was a period referred to by some historians as the 'domestication' of the RIC, when civil duties predominated and the semi-military aspects of the police receded. This may be one of the reasons behind the unpreparedness of the force when faced with the challenge that came in the wake of the 1916 Easter Rising in Dublin. After the execution of their leaders, a wave of sympathy swept the country and saw Sinn Fein sweep to power in the general election of 1918. With calls for all-Ireland parliaments, and to boycott the British state and its institutions, the police in every town and village became a convenient focus for resentment. Boycotts led to the first murder of police by the new Irish Republican Army (IRA) in 1919 when two officers were killed whilst escorting a load of explosives for quarry use in Co Tipperary.

Michael Collins, leader of the IRA, identified the single greatest strength of the RIC to be its local intelligence network and famously called each station, 'the eyes and ears of Dublin Castle'. He directed his columns to destroy the smaller rural stations to force the police to withdraw from such areas into larger, better protected stations, thus denying them local knowledge.

The RIC, having been used to many years of relative peace, were unprepared for the violent onslaught of such attacks and many older men used the opportunity to resign. The deteriorating security situation and need for manpower led to the decision to recruit ex-British army officers and other ranks into the RIC, in either the RIC Auxiliary Division (for ex-officers) or into stations directly (known as 'Black and Tans' for other ranks); hardened by trench warfare and with little local knowledge or sympathy, these often made police relations with local communities worse, although in the case of the auxiliary division they proved highly effective against the IRA 'flying columns'.

In the north of Ireland, the 'Troubles' took on a sectarian flavour, especially in Belfast where there were clashes in 'flashpoint' areas between working-class nationalists and unionist communities. Catholics were forced from workplaces, such as the shipyards and linen mills, because of a perceived sympathy with the activities of the IRA in the rest of Ireland. A unit of the IRA formed in Belfast in response and the city endured the disorder of gun-battles, sniping, assassinations, and arson attacks. The British army was called out and Belfast placed under military curfew until 1924.

Another northern development was the recruitment of a force of Special Constabulary from the wider unionist community from 1920 to act as an auxiliary police in support of the RIC. This force was to swell enormously in the period of 1920 to 1922 and took over most of the routine security duties from the RIC.

A truce was finally declared in July 1921 after nearly 700 members of the RIC had been killed over the previous two years of violence. The subsequent agreement on the partition of the island marked the end of the RIC as an all-Ireland force and it was officially disbanded on 31 May 1922.

Royal Irish Constabulary station plate, Queen Victoria Crown.

Constabulary party at Carnlough, 1875.

The men are wearing the 'postman's shako' worn from 1874 and carry long sword bayonets. A Sub Inspector stands on the far left, beside whom is a mounted trooper.

Constabulary party *c.* 1875.

RIC head-dress.
Shown are 'postman's shako' (1874–1883) on left and officer's helmet (1883–1922) on right.

RIC group with District Inspector Thomas St George McCarthy, 1883.
DI McCarthy was a founding member of the Gaelic Athletic Association (GAA) when stationed at Templemore.

THE RIOTS IN BELFAST.

THE POLICE CHARGING THE MOB IN THE BRICKFIELDS.

THE CONSTABULARY ENTERING THE ORANGE DISTRICT, SHANKHILL-ROAD.

Belfast Riots, 1886, from the *Illustrated London News.*

Belfast suffered serious sectarian disorder at the time of the first Home Rule Bill for Ireland in 1886.

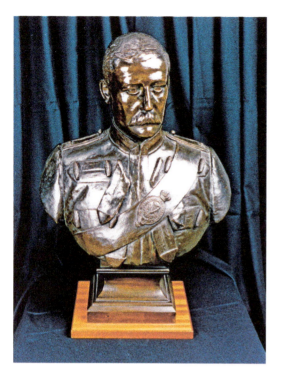

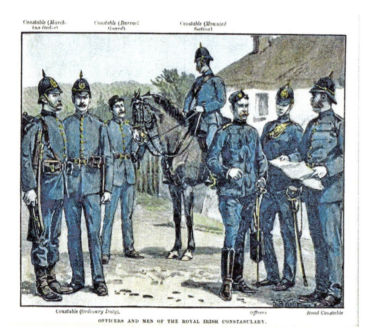

Constable (March-
ing Order).

Constable (Barrack
Guard).

Constable (Mounted
Section).

Constable (Ordinary Duty).

Officers

Head Constable

OFFICERS AND MEN OF THE ROYAL IRISH CONSTABULARY.

Above left: Bronze bust of District Inspector William Limerick Martin, 1889. District Inspector Martin was attacked and killed by a crowd whilst attempting to arrest a priest during disturbances in Donegal in 1889.

Above right: Silver candelabra from RIC officers' mess at Phoenix Park depot.

Left: RIC ranks and uniforms *c.* 1890.

RIC on eviction duty *c.* 1890.

Constable A. McGladdery at Ballyclare Fair *c.* 1890.

RIC station party, Swanlinbar, Co Cavan, 1892.
Note the 'penny farthing' bicycles and Head Constable with four chevrons.

RIC World Champion 'tug-of-war' team, 1893.

Above left: RIC group in 'full-marching order' with packs and Snider carbines *c.* 1895.
This equipment would have been carried when policing riots or disorder.

Above right: RIC group at Musgrave Street station, Belfast *c.* 1895.
The two figures on either side of the back row are plain-clothes detectives.

Below: RIC Mounted Troop, 1897.
Mounted troop on the square at the Phoenix Park Depot before their departure to take part in Queen Victoria's Diamond Jubilee Parade in London.

Sergeant Ballantine in cycling uniform, County Donegal, 1898, with illuminated address presented to him, Falcarragh, Co Donegal, 1899.
Addresses of this kind were often presented to officers and men on transfer as a mark of esteem from local communities.

Left: Constables outside station in Belfast *c.* 1900.
The Constable on the right is dressed for winter duty in greatcoat with woollen gloves. They both wear numerals – or 'borough numbers' – on their collar (only worn by men serving in Belfast, Londonderry, and Cork City).

Below: RIC volunteers serving with Lord Iveagh's Hospital Corps during the Boer War, 1900.

Above left: Sergeants from British West Africa police forces in training with the RIC in Dublin *c.* 1900.

Above right: Colonel Sir Neville Chamberlain, Inspector General, 1900–1916.

RIC Constables in De Dion-Bouton vis-á-vis motor car *c.* 1903.

School of instruction at RIC Depot, 1903.
A plaster-cast of a footprint is being shown to the class. Note the sectioned model house used for instruction in investigating burglaries and copper and worm from a poteen still on far left for instruction in illicit distillation.

Belfast police van at Musgrave Street c. 1905.

Station party paraded for formal inspection at Musgrave Street, Belfast, 1906.
Photograph shows the first appearance of the Belfast RIC band, seen at the rear.

RIC escorting transport vehicles during the Belfast transport strike of 1907.

RIC escort for Corpus Christi procession *c.* 1910.

Police with stolen purses at Celtic Park, Belfast, 1911.

The police are holding wallets and purses stolen and emptied by pickpockets on the occasion of Winston Churchill's visit to Belfast to talk in favour of Home Rule for Ireland.

Above: First batch of RIC recruits for Irish Guards during the First World War at Guards Depot, London, in December 1914.

Left: RIC mounted troop escorting military funeral *c.* 1915.

Ford Model 'T' tender at Phoenix Park, 1917. This was the first motor transport acquired by the RIC. Note small RIC crest on bodywork.

Mixed RIC/British Army cycle patrol *c.* 1920. Photographed at Clonakilty, Co Cork. Note the naval rating in the background. Larger stations were equipped with a radio manned by Royal Navy operators.

Lord French inspecting members of the RIC Auxiliary Division, 1920/21. Lord French was Lord Lieutenant of Ireland and is seen inspecting Auxiliaries at Phoenix Park.

To Wish you Happiness this
Christmas-tide and through
the Coming Year

From

THE NEW R.I.C. *1921-1922.*

Image from an RIC Christmas card *c.* 1921.
Showing (from left to right), an RIC Constable, a 'Black and Tan' (British ex-soldier serving in the RIC), an officer cadet from the RIC Auxiliary Division, and a members of the Veterans' Corps (a force of ex-police and military carrying out limited security duties).

1836 CONSTABULARY 1922
IN MEMORY OF
THE ROYAL IRISH
CONSTABULARY AND
OF THE OFFICERS
AND MEN WHO FELL
IN THE DISCHARGE
OF DUTY DURING
THE EXISTENCE OF
THE FORCE AND IN
THE GREAT WAR
1914-1918

Above left: March-past of last RIC detachment at evacuation of RIC Depot, Phoenix Park, Dublin, 1922.

Above right: Memorial tablet to the Officers and Men of the Royal Irish Constabulary, St Paul's Cathedral, London.

The Ulster Special Constabulary

The Ulster Special Constabulary (USC) had its roots in the turmoil which engulfed Ireland from 1919. The activities of the IRA in the north of Ireland and demand for protection from its people led the British administration in Dublin to authorise the establishment of an auxiliary police force to support the hard-pressed RIC. Recruiting began in Belfast in November 1920 and soon spread to other northern counties and comprised three classes: 'A', which was full-time; 'B', which was part-time; 'C', which comprised over-age members available for emergencies only in their local areas.

Much of the recruiting mirrored the organisation of the Ulster Volunteer Force (UVF) and many 'Specials' were former members of this force. From the start, the majority of recruits came from a Protestant unionist background and this was to colour the image of the Special Constabulary for the entire period of its existence. Many of the first members wore civilian clothes and were armed with smuggled former-UVF rifles.

Acting as a force in support, first of the RIC and later the RUC, the USC carried out a range of police duties, but mainly those of a security nature; patrolling, guard duties, and carrying out security checks. The force proved invaluable in ensuring the security of the new Northern Ireland in its early days and the first police casualties of the state were USC members.

Although the force came under the control of the RUC Inspector General, the force had its own command and training structure separate from that of the regular police and was organised by county and sub-districts below this. Due to its primarily security-based role, it maintained a semi-military nature, which led many of its officer ranks to be filled by retired British army officers The conclusion of the Irish Civil War, the improved security situation and the cost of maintaining its numbers led to a drastic reduction in the size of the USC and after 1925 only one class – the part-time 'B' – remained.

Over time the 'B Specials' became part of Ulster life in nearly every town and village and became, in a time of limited leisure activities, perceived by some as providing an element of local social activity for the Protestant community. Members attended weekly drills and routine exercises and in rural areas kept their rifles at home in case of emergency. A major aspect of service for members of the force was small bore pistol and rifle shooting for which there was keen competition at local and national levels.

In urban areas members of the force wore the standard RUC uniform and carried side arms, whereas in rural areas they wore the First World War British army pattern service dress dyed black and carried rifles.

The USC worked closely with the RUC and even shared some of the larger stations. As it served under its own officers, it operated in support of the RUC. It remained a key part of the Unionist government's security structure and in rural areas its members provided local knowledge and intelligence on nationalist and republican activities. The attitude towards the force and its members by the nationalist community was at best ambivalent and at worse hostile.

The USC was available to be mobilised in support of the RUC in emergencies, such as during the Second World War and the IRA 'Border Campaign' of 1956–62. As a readily-armed and organised force, the USC provided the foundation and nucleus of the Ulster Home Guard during the Second World War.

The force remained part-time apart from a small cadre of administrative and training staff and as there was no compulsory retirement age for the force until 1968, it was common to find members in the 1960s who had served since the inception of the force.

As late as 1969, it retained a paper strength of 10,000 members; however, it was not deployed in any large numbers to deal with the disturbances that erupted in that year. Due to its perceived partisanship in being drawn from the Protestant and Unionist community, there was also a reluctance to use the force in nationalist areas where its presence might inflame matters.

The force was disbanded under the terms of the Hunt Report on policing reform on 30 April 1970 and was replaced jointly by the RUC's own part-time reserve and the Ulster Defence Regiment.

Early detachment of the Special Constabulary *c.* 1921.
A shortage of uniforms meant many early members were only issued police caps and raincoats and were armed with ex-UVF rifles.

Early 'B Special' party outside RIC station *c.* 1921.

'Specials' with a Lancia 'cage car' manning a piquet on Royal Avenue, Belfast, 1922.

Special Constabulary recruiting party about to leave Castle Barracks, Enniskillen *c.* 1922.

'C' class Specials, Albertbridge Road, East Belfast, 1922. Note the civilian clothes worn and ex-UVF rifles carried.

Claudy 'Specials' lining a bank, 1922. Note the Lewis light machine gun and rifle with grenade-firing adaption.

Special Constabulary lying in ambush near the border c. 1922.

'Specials' building a breastwork entrenchment, 1922.

Party of rural 'Specials' with Crossley tender outside base *c.* 1923.

'Specials' on patrol in a Crossley tender on the border, 1922.

Firearm certificate issued to 'B Special' in 1922, enabling rifle to be kept at home.

'B' class Special Constabulary on parade at Dromore, Co Tyrone, for Lord Derby's visit, April 1923.
Lord Derby, British Secretary of State for War, visited Northern Ireland in April 1923 to inspect security arrangements.

'B' class Special Constabulary Guard of Honour for Governor's state entry to Londonderry, 5 May 1923.

'Specials' moving to take up defensive positions alongside border road *c.* 1922.

Special Constabulary band.

The Governor's Guard inspected by H. G. Duke of Abercorn *c.* 1935.

The Governor's Guard was the personal guard for the H. G. Duke of Abercorn when Governor of Northern Ireland from 1922 until 1945.

They were stationed at the Governor's official residence of Hillsborough Castle and at the Duke's residence at Baronscourt in Co Tyrone. It was drawn from ex-servicemen members of the USC and was under the command of Captain Martelli (an ex-member of the RIC Auxiliary Division).

Members wore monogrammed shoulder badges with letters 'GG,' green aiglets, and black leather bandoliers.

Right: Governor's Guard tunic.
Note the nine pouch bandolier, green aiglet, and 'GG' monogrammed shoulder badge.

Below: A series of still images from an Ulster Home Guard (UHG) recruitment film delivered by Major-General Majendie, CB, DSO, GOC NID.
Bottom left – UHG ambush an 'enemy' vehicle.
Bottom right – Major-General Majendie taking the salute from a column of UHG.

Members of Newcastle UHG engage the 'invader' in realistic battle scenes, which were enacted to inaugurate Home Guard recruiting week at Newcastle, Co Down.

Members of Dromara Platoon, UHG, on training exercises near the 'white rocks' in the Dromara Hills, Co Down. (Howard Hamilton)
In the background is their platoon transport; a Morris PU truck.
From left to right, front row: A. Baird, Lieutenant J. Ferguson, G. Archer, E. McCollum.
Middle row: J. Rogers, A. Guiney, R. Dewart, Captain R. Ferguson.
Back row: W. Dewart, V. Stewart.

Platoon (Clough/Seaforde), 2 Down Battalion. (Down County Museum)

At the creation of the Local Defence Volunteers (LDV), Seaforde USC moved drill halls to the minor hall at Clough Presbyterian Church. The photograph was taken on the steps of Downpatrick Courthouse on the day of the Stand Down Parade in Downpatrick, 3 December 1944.

From left to right, back row: John Jennings Jnr, Hugh W. Croskery, Stanley Hill, -? , John McAnally, John Fitz, R. Watson, Tom Ash, A. Dixon.

Middle row: Norman Robinson, John Kennedy, David Gillespie, George Newell, Jim Strain, William Casement, William Shanks, William Blakely, Jack Wright.

Front row: Jack McBride, William Blue, Charlie Jennings, Jack Kennedy, John Jennings Snr, Herbie Jennings, Matt Kilpatrick, Charlie Fitzpatrick, Desmond Logan.

Members of the USC, 'B' Category, undergoing training on a rifle range.

USC Ballintoy platoon with shooting trophies, 1960.

USC shooting champions with Lord Brookeborough, Prime Minister of Northern Ireland, 1960.

The Royal Ulster Constabulary

The Royal Ulster Constabulary came into being on 1 June 1922 under the jurisdiction of the new Unionist government of Northern Ireland. Due to the turbulent period of its birth it remained a semi-military force with the role of protecting Northern Ireland from armed subversion. The new government was concerned that Britain might abandon Northern Ireland or that it might be invaded by the new Irish Free State, aided and abetted by the IRA. Due to this, the government insisted on strong policing powers embodied in the Civil Authorities Special Powers Act; a temporary measure, later made permanent, by which the government had the right to arrest without warrant, or imprison without trial anyone thought to be a threat to the state. This was directed against Irish nationalism or republicanism.

The new RUC was 3,000 strong, backed up by a Special Constabulary, initially full-time but later part-time in the 'B' class, 8–10,000 strong. These were available to be mobilised on a full-time basis in periods of crisis, such as during the war years or during periodic IRA campaigns in the north.

Many serving RIC men in the north continued into the new RUC and the new force offered places to any ex-RIC members. The new force initially comprised half ex-RIC. Due to this, the percentage of Catholic officers was initially 23 per cent. However, this fell as those ex-RIC gradually retired until it reached 9 per cent; a figure that remained largely unchanged until the end of the RUC in 2001.

As the situation stabilised in Northern Ireland the RUC developed a range of specialised functions, such as a Fingerprints Branch in 1923 and a Traffic Branch in 1930.

The RUC was under the direct control of the Unionist Minister for Home Affairs and such political control was to compromise its actions at a later period.

Many of the dilapidated rented stations inherited from the RIC were replaced by a new-look rural station design from 1930. These became known as the 'Rippingham' pattern stations after their architect.

The IRA lay dormant for long periods. However, the first RUC man to be killed was in 1933 when Constable John Ryan was killed during an IRA bank raid. Short-lived IRA campaigns were launched during the Second World War and in border areas in 1956 to 1962.

Rising nationalist expectations and demonstrations after the Second World War necessitated the formation of a Reserve Force in 1950, trained to deal with public order events. Mobile and radio equipped, they were increasingly involved in policing street demonstrations and were used against the IRA during the 'Border' campaign.

A modernisation programme was launched in the 1960s, whereby many older stations were closed and others turned into limited opening stations, open only certain days of the week. The concept of mobile patrolling was introduced, whereby each station would have a radio-equipped car or small motorcycle to improve patrolling efficiency.

The terms and conditions of service were improved, although single officers were still required to live in barracks and a set working week and overtime had to wait until the late 1960s.

A Women's Section was set up in 1943 to deal with crime related to women and children, although the numbers of female officers remained small and they tended to be posted only to larger urban stations. Women were not fully integrated into the RUC until the 1970s and had to wait until 1994 for full parity when they were allowed to carry firearms for the first time.

The Civil Rights movement started in the 1960s, calling for equal rights for all and, copying the model of non-violent protest, saw marches and sit-downs in Belfast, Londonderry, and other towns. These marches led to Unionist counter-marches aimed at maintaining the status quo. Many in the unionist government saw the hand of the IRA in this movement and the RUC were caught in the middle, between increasingly violent protests and government directives to deal robustly with protestors. This tension led to widespread rioting in 1968 and 1969, which stretched the manpower of the RUC to the limit and led to the need of Stormont to call on Westminster for assistance from the British army to help restore order.

A major reform of the RUC followed in 1969–70, which saw its paramilitary duties and equipment taken from it, the establishment of the Police Authority for Northern Ireland to be responsible for the police, the disbandment of the Special Constabulary and its replacement by the RUC's part-time reserve, and the disarming of the force. This was carried out against the background of a deteriorating security situation, as the new Provisional IRA appeared in 1969 and killed its first officers in Crossmaglen in 1970.

The British army was given primacy for security decisions and relations between the army and local RUC was often poor and even acrimonious in the early 1970s.

A policy of 'police primacy' was finally adopted in 1976, whereby the job of security was transferred to the RUC, backed up by the army only when requested. A result of this was an increase in the numbers of police, a Full-Time Reserve introduced in 1974, and increased investment in vehicles and technology to combat the terrorist threat. The size of the force peaked at 13,000 by 2000, comprising regular RUC and Full- and Part-Time Reserve Officers.

A Community Affairs branch was set up in 1970; the first in the UK, aimed at improving community relations, mainly through youth focussed activities. On the other side of the coin, the RUC's public order capability was improved with the establishment of the Special Patrol Group (SPG) to replace the RUC's earlier Reserve Force, later District Mobile Support Units (DMSUs), Mobile Support Units (MSUs), and Tactical Support Group (TSG).

The security situation of the 1970s and 1980s meant that police had to be heavily armed and protected, wearing flak jackets and patrolling in armoured Land Rovers. The stresses of police life increased dramatically due the constant threat to officers and their families, both on and off duty.

Confidence in the RUC fell amongst the broad nationalist community due to a series of controversies; the use of 'Supergrasses' in the 1970s, the alleged 'shoot to kill policy' in border areas, and allegations of collusion with loyalist paramilitaries in the 1980s. Members of the force were attacked by members of the unionist community for the first time after their policing of protests against the Anglo-Irish agreement of 1985.

The ceasefires of the early 1990s and signing of the Belfast or 'Good Friday' agreement in 1998 led to a call for policing reform. The British government set up a commission under politician Chris Patten to examine policing models for Northern Ireland. His findings echoed what had occurred in South Africa a decade before, when the old pre-apartheid police force – which had been primarily a state security force – was reformed by a process of gradual reform rather than whole-scale disbandment. This led to the setting up of the Police Service of Northern Ireland on 4 November 2001, which incorporated the former Royal Ulster Constabulary.

In recognition of its collective gallantry in policing the Northern Ireland 'Troubles,' the RUC was awarded the George Cross by Her Majesty The Queen in April 2000; the only other such award being to the people of the island of Malta during the Second World War.

In the course of the 'Troubles' from 1969 to 2001, 302 officers were killed as a result of terrorist activity.

Original RUC 'Red Hand' pattern cap and collar badges.
This design using the red hand of Ulster on a St George's Cross was originally used by the RUC from 1922, but due to its unpopularity with the force was soon dropped in favour of the traditional RUC 'Harp and Crown' design.

Lancia 'cage-car' manned by Special Constabulary *c.* 1923.

RUC Lancia 'cage-car' with crew responding to an incident in Belfast city centre *c.* 1923.

RUC Rolls-Royce armoured cars, Belfast *c.* 1935.

"AT THE BORDER." CUSTOMS EXAMINATION STATION BETWEEN NORTHERN IRELAND AND THE IRISH FREE STATE.

RUC on customs duty on the Northern Ireland/Irish Free State border *c.* 1930.

Lancia 'cage-car' and crew, Marine Street (off York Road), Belfast, 1935.
The cage protection was to deflect missiles being thrown into the vehicle. Note the rifles carried and the loyalist flags and bunting in the background.

The image was taken during the serious rioting that occurred in the city on the occasion of the Silver Jubilee of King George V.

Interior of hut at RUC Depot Newtownards c. 1925.
The Newtownards Depot was a First World War-era hutted camp, which was occupied by the RUC in 1922 and used for training until 1936. Note the spartan living conditions and military furniture.

Recruits at drill at Newtownards Depot *c.* 1925.
Note the band on the left and wooden huts, which comprised the camp, and grass drill square.

RUC Traffic Branch, 1930.
Triumph motorcycles and sidecars were the first vehicles used by Traffic after its establishment in 1930.

Illicit still seized at Landhead, Ballymoney, 1926.

Constable Stewart Patterson on tillage duty on Rathlin Island 1950.
The RUC carried out the annual agricultural census on behalf of the Ministry of Agriculture called tillage duty.

Right: RUC Dungannon *c.* 1965.
Dungannon station was built originally as an RIC barracks in 1870 for the RIC in the Scottish baronial style and had a sister station in Cahirciveen in Co Kerry.

There was a popular myth that a government department mixed up designs for police stations in India and Ireland, which led to the design of the two North-West Frontier stations being used in Ireland while two Irish-style whitewashed slate-roofed country stations were built in India.

Below: Cartoon from *Constabulary Gazette* showing RUC boxing contests against German police team, 1934.
Note the Nazi swastika worn by the German boxers. 'Jimmy' Magill, the renowned RUC boxer of the 1930s/40s, is also featured.

RUC Training Centre Enniskillen, aerial view *c.* 1980.

First RUC Women's Section squad, Enniskillen 1944.

Right: RUC party on duty at '*feis*' *c.* 1948. Note the ex-army short-wave radio being used. District Inspector R. Spears, ex-RAF, seen on right (note the pilot's wings unofficially worn).

Below: Recruits at revolver practice, Enniskillen *c.* 1950.

RUC Reserve Force on parade for the Inspector General, Sir Richard Pim KBE, VRD, DL, RNVR at Ballykinler, 1950.

RUC District Inspector and Sergeant specially mounted as escort for the Prime Minister of Northern Ireland in the coronation procession, 1953.

Recruits at RUC Depot Enniskillen wearing denim overalls worn in training, 1955.

Driving school at RUC Depot, Enniskillen.
The cars shown are Humber Hawks.

RUC vehicle check during IRA 'Border Campaign', 1958.

Reserve Force vehicles at Moneymore during IRA 'Border Campaign', 1958.
Note the White half-track leased from the British army.

Above: RUC officers embarking for patrol on army helicopter *c.* 1958.

Right: £5,000 reward notice regarding the murder of Sergeant A. J. Ovens, 1957. Sergeant Ovens was killed by an IRA booby-trap bomb when searching an empty house in Coalisland.

MURDER
£5,000 REWARD

A reward of £5,000 will be paid by the Government of Northern Ireland to any person who furnishes information leading to the arrest and conviction of one or more of the persons responsible for the murder of

SERGEANT ARTHUR JAMES OVENS,
Royal Ulster Constabulary,
near Coalisland, Co. Tyrone, on 17th August, 1957.

Information may be supplied in STRICT CONFIDENCE to The Inspector General, Royal Ulster Constabulary Headquarters, Belfast, Telephone No. Belfast 25421, any Police Station, or any member of the Force.

September, 1957.

Above: RUC Helen's Bay, Co Down *c.* 1965.

Helen's Bay was an example of the small RUC sub stations constructed in the late 1950s as semi-detached dwelling houses/offices for officers and their families. Note the Velocette LE lightweight motorcycle for patrol duties, used by many UK forces at the time.

Left: New open-neck RUC uniform as worn by Head Constable, Sergeant, and Constable.

Note the leather cross-strap worn by the Sergeant and Constable to support the revolver, which was discontinued in 1963.

RUC Ford Zephyr Mk II estate *c.* 1961.
The white livery was used for motorway patrol work. Note the tall radio aerial, loudspeaker, and ice sensor mounted on the front bumper.

RUC patrol car, Ford Zephyr Mk III, with two officers investigating the site of a road traffic accident, Knock Road, Belfast *c.* 1966.

Motorist's view of being stopped by a 'Q' car *c.* 1965. Note the drop-down stop sign.

"Wait till I tell ya young fella!!"

Rowel Friers cartoon of life in the RUC, 1960s.
The cartoon shows a new young officer – who is dreaming of 'space-age' policing – listening to an old retired member who is relating the realities of life in a border station with long hours, arduous duties, and basic amenities.

Constables being briefed for night duty at Donegall Pass station, 1966.
They are wearing the distinctive 'night-hat' worn for city night patrolling until 1969.

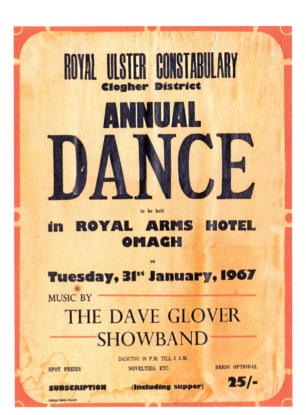

Right: Poster advertising RUC Clogher District dance, 1967. Many RUC districts organised regular dances featuring the popular Irish showbands of the day.

Below: RUC officer on fire from petrol bomb attack during riots in Londonderry, 1969.

Above: RUC providing protection to Civil Rights marchers at Burntollet Bridge, Co Londonderry, in January 1969.

Left: The changing face of Rathfriland station, before and after the start of the 'Troubles', 1965 and 1985.

Opposite above: RUC Victoria, Londonderry *c.* 1975.
Victoria station was built for the RIC and opened as the city's main station in 1883. An RUC Constable and soldier are seen on guard duty shortly before its closure in 1975.

Opposite below left: RUC Reserve recruiting poster, 1971.

Opposite below right: RUC Cadet Scheme recruiting poster *c.* 1977.

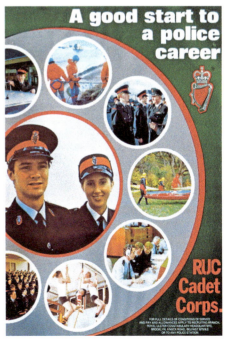

Today's RUC

A career in the Royal Ulster Constabulary.

Left: RUC recruiting brochure 1973.

Below: RUC Ford Cortina Mk II *c.* 1970. This district/sub-divisional car is shown with its road traffic accident equipment deployed.

RUC officer giving advice to schoolchildren, Enniskillen *c.* 1975.

Members of RUC Special Patrol Group existing from Land Rover *c.* 1977.

RUC officer on patrol with rifle, Belfast *c.* 1990.

RUC New Barnsley *c.* 1985.
This station in west Belfast was under frequent terrorist attack and was nicknamed 'Fort Apache.'

RUC Mobile Support Unit forming shield wall *c.* 1985.
Note the shield held above heads to provide protection from missiles and baton round gun.

RUC officers alighting from a Tangi Landrover in the late 1980s.

RUC armoured Ford Cortina Mk V at Musgrave Street *c.* 1984.

RUC Constable on cycle patrol at Carrickfergus Castle *c.* 1982.

Left: RUC officer's mess dress jacket and waistcoat *c.* 1982. Officers of the rank of Inspector and above were allowed to wear mess dress when attending official functions until 2001.

Below: RUC/army vehicle checkpoint *c.* 1990.

RUC Traffic Branch vehicles, 1988.
Ford Granadas with an unmarked Ford Capri and BMW R80 motorcycle.

Visit of HRH The Duchess of Kent to RUC Headquarters, 1989.

Left: Piper, RUC Band *c.* 1995.

Below: RUC Air Support Islander aircraft *c.* 1995.

RUC officers boarding army Chinook helicopter for duty during Drumcree protests, 1995/96.

RUC officers at ease during Drumcree protests, 1995/96.

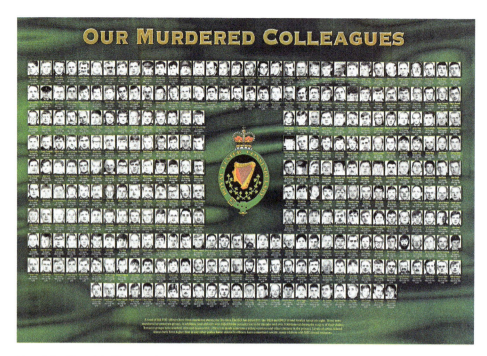

'Our Murdered Colleagues' poster.
Poster produced as memorial to 300 RUC officers killed by terrorist activity from 1969 to 2001.

Award of George Cross to RUC by HM The Queen, 2001.

The Police Service of Northern Ireland

The Police (Northern Ireland) Act 2000 established a new police force for Northern Ireland – The Police Service of Northern Ireland (incorporating the Royal Ulster Constabulary), which came into being on 4 November 2001.

Some of the most controversial aspects of the act were the dropping of the Royal prefix, the removal of the Union Flag from police stations, and a policy of 50/50 recruiting from Catholic and Protestant (and other) backgrounds with the aim of making the service more representative of the community as a whole and raising the percentage of Catholic officers, which in 2011 stood at only 9 per cent. This proved a success and by 2011 over 30 per cent of officers came from a Catholic background.

To promote a neutral working environment national symbols have been removed from uniforms and insignia; the use of embroidered shamrocks on Sergeants' chevrons and the cap bands of senior ranks were discontinued and the Royal Crown was removed from the insignia of senior ranks. A new PSNI badge was introduced to reflect both historical traditions in Northern Ireland, whilst also displaying symbols of justice, peace, and truth.

The respect for human rights has become paramount in all police training and work and many former military type aspects of student training have been abolished. The training course for student officers is now accredited to national standards by the University of Ulster and the former Oath of Allegiance to the Crown has been replaced by an affirmation.

On an organisational level, the former police divisions and sub-divisions were replaced with twenty-nine District Command Units (DCUs) intended to be broadly in line with the local council areas. There has been subsequent reorganisation of these in recent years.

To make the new service more flexible, more policing and budgetary powers have been devolved to local districts, where local officers work with local residents in District Policing Partnerships.

The PSNI is accountable to a wide range of national and international agencies. This has included the Oversight Commissioner who was appointed to ensure that the Patten recommendations were implemented 'comprehensively and faithfully', and attempted to assure the community that all aspects of the report were being implemented and being seen to be implemented. The oversight role ended on 31 May 2007, with the final report indicating that of Patten's 175 recommendations, 140 had been completed with a further 16 'substantially completed'.

Under the act the Police Authority for Northern Ireland was replaced by the NI Policing Board and in January 2007 Sinn Fein joined the Policing Board and have been members ever since.

A further landmark for the PSNI came in April 2010 when policing and justice powers were devolved to Northern Ireland for the first time since 1972.

Approval of the new service amongst the nationalist community received a major boost when in 2002 the GAA (Gaelic Athletic Association) ended its century-long ban on members of the police and British military from playing Gaelic sport.

A developing security problem has been that of dissident republican terrorist activity aimed at disrupting the peace process in Northern Ireland and the threat level to police officers remains. Several have been murdered since the inception of the service.

The PSNI officer in many ways faces the same challenges as did earlier 'Peelers'; of policing a divided society with the threat of political/religious violence – a challenge faced today by many other colleagues throughout the world.

RUC GC Foundation Garden opened in 2003 has received a number of prestigious architectural and gardening awards.

Aughnacloy PSNI station, refurbished in line with the Patten recommendations to give it a more welcoming, 'user-friendly' appearance, February 2005.

Police holding a scene after an attempted murder, Londonderry, 2007.

PSNI restrain loyalist protesters from clashing with republican counter-protesters during an Armed Forces Thanksgiving Parade in Belfast, November 2008.

A TSG shield line at Ardoyne shop fronts, Belfast, under attack from fireworks, July 2009.

Above: PSNI boat patrol at Tall Ships Maritime Festival, Belfast, August 2009.

Right: PSNI officers on a neighbourhood patrol, 2006.

Cap and tunic of the former PSNI Deputy Chief Constable Judith Gillespie.
Judith Gillespie is the most senior female officer to date and retired in March 2014 after thirty-two years' service with both the RUC and PSNI.

Police 44 rescuing local people from the snow around Plumbridge, March 2010.

Chief Constable Matt Baggott and President of Ireland Mary McAleese at the graduation of PSNI Student Officers, August 2010.

Evidence gathering at the scene of a security alert in North Belfast, February 2011.

PSNI officers under attack by rioters at Ardoyne, Belfast, July 2011.

The Road and Armed Support Unit Project Evo car, followed by motorcycle outriders at St Patrick's Day Parade, Downpatrick.

PSNI Officers patrolling on bicycles, Belfast, 2004.

Police officer updating the district Facebook page whilst on patrol, December 2012.

The helicopters of the PSNI Air Support Unit, January 2013.

Chief Inspector G. Dodds and Reserve Constable Robinson QPM at street celebrations to mark Tyrone winning the All Ireland Senior Football Championship in Ballygawley, 2003.

Deputy Chief Constable Judith Gillespie and Dame Mary Peters at the World Police and Fire Games in Belfast, August 2013.

The PSNI memorial garden built to commemorate PSNI officers who lost their lives in service of the people of Northern Ireland has won several awards from the Royal Institute of British Architects, July 2014.

Sponsored armoured Landrover pull by O1 TSG to raise funds for young people in 'A' District to participate in a community learning programme in South Africa, June 2014.

PSNI officers getting ready for the *Giro d'Italia* held throughout Ireland, July 2014.

PSNI community policing, 2004.

Right: PSNI Student Officers celebrate the end of their graduation parade, October 2014.

Below: PSNI Pipes and Drum leading the funeral procession for PC Dave Phillips, Merseyside Police, in October 2015.

Joint Irish (PSNI and AGS) Police rugby team play an English Police team at Newforge, Belfast, March 2016.

Downpatrick PSNI station won the Sustainable Building of the Year Award, November 2016. The PSNI was praised for its incorporation of a wide range of sustainable features in the building and its design, such as natural cooling and heating, sedum roofs, rainwater recovery, and a sustainable urban drainage system to reduce storm water run-off.

Other Antecedent and Related Forces

Londonderry Borough Police (1849 to 1870)

In the city of Derry – or Londonderry – the old Corporation had set up a night watch, which proved to be so ineffective that the citizens had engaged their own representatives or carried out the duties themselves. In 1832 a Police Committee was formed which improved the situation. Despite the appointment of a Head Constable and twelve Constables, the growth of the town meant that by the middle of the next decade it was inadequate to the task in hand. A new Corporation was formed in 1841 and set about lobbying MPs to create legislation to assist with improvements. The Londonderry Improvement Act 1849 empowered the Corporation to deal with the problems of water supply, sewage, street surfacing, markets, police, lighting and so on.

The Londonderry Borough Police was established in 1849 when the police committee decided on 'the establishment of a day and night police upon the same footing as in other large towns' and took advice from the London Metropolitan Police, which seconded a Sergeant James Wilson to organise the new force. It had an initial strength of twenty-one constables; thirteen for day and eight for night duties, two sergeants, and one Superintendent. The initial cost, including uniforms, was £680 per annum. The men wore frock coats, top hats with bone reinforcement, and carried lamps, rattles, and batons. Two local nicknames are recorded for them by various sources; the 'Horny Dicks' – possibly due to the bone reinforcements in their top hats – and the 'Bang Beggars'.

In addition to the preservation of the peace, life, and property, the police carried out of other duties such as fire-fighting and sanitary duties.

Their areas of jurisdiction were fixed: 'on the north – Mrs Young's stores, Strand Road; on the west – Mr Smyth's Gate Casino; the Waterside included, beyond the bridge and the Infirmary Gate'.

There police availed of premises in Market Street owned by Andrew Clarke up until 1863, when they moved to East Wall, which was owned by Isaac Colhoun. Colhoun is listed as having premises that were used by the police on Shipquay Street until 1883, where he had a legal practice and land agency. The Shipquay barracks were roughly where Jefferson Court/Casey & Company is situated today.

Being regulated by the Londonderry Corporation, the Borough police were governed by the Police and Markets Committee 'To Supervise regulate and direct the working of the police force'. According to the Corporation's Quarterly Reports, the main issue that dominated was the problem of constables intoxicated whilst on duty – a problem not confined only to the Londonderry police.

Jan–May 1860
'Constable James Young, charged by the Superintendent of police for being intoxicated whilst on duty on the night of the twenty seventh November was fined five shillings'.

November 1860
'Police Constable James Young reported for being intoxicated and disorderly whilst on duty on the morning of the twenty ninth September last, was fined twenty shillings and his dismissal has been ordered in case of a repetition of the offence'.

February 1861
'Constable Daniel Barr charged with intoxication whilst on duty on the twenty ninth of October last was ordered to pay a fine of five shillings'.

'Constable Samuel Smith for being intoxicated and sleeping in Egg Box at the Waterside, whilst on duty on the morning of the eighth of November last was ordered to pay a fine of twenty shillings with the authority to the Mayor to dismiss him for any future offences'.

'Supernumerary Patrick Doherty reported for being intoxicated whilst on duty on the sixteenth of January was dismissed'.

In the face of an increasing number of sectarian riots in the city, the Borough Police were hampered by their small size, inadequate training, lack of firearms, and poor discipline.

During a visit by Prince Arthur to Londonderry on 28 April 1869, the police fired upon the crowds of rioting sectarian factions. As a consequence, two apprentice boys were killed, with many more people injured. Following this, the government directed an inquiry into the rioting, headed by two barristers and, by the second week in May, the borough was proclaimed under the Peace Preservation Act.

In July 1869 Sir Hervey Bruce questioned in the House of Commons why the proclamation was still in place as there was little evidence of criminality and the coroner had found that the populace were not responsible for the loss of the life, and that it was indeed the police who were responsible. The government's reply was that there were arms held by a section of the city who were 'angry and excited'. It was then questioned whether the Londonderry police were fit for purpose:

All this showed that throughout Ireland there was a want of vigilance and efficiency on the part of the police. Individually, and for the purposes to which they were put, the police were admirable; but what was daily occurring constituted an irrefragable proof that they were not sufficient or properly organized to maintain the authority of the law. If the state of the city of

Londonderry had been known to the police, they ought not to have allowed a Royal Prince to go there without taking due precautions for the preservation of the peace.

Marquis of Clanricarde.

The Lord Lieutenant on 11 August 1869 ordered a commission to investigate policing in Londonderry. The findings of the commission were that the policing arrangements in the city required complete alteration and that the 'police force maintained by the town council of the borough of Londonderry should cease to exist'. It also noted, but did not endorse, allegations that the borough police discriminated against Roman Catholics. The upshot of these findings were that the existing legislation pertaining to the Royal Irish Constabulary was amended in the guise of the Constabulary (Ireland) Amendment Act 1870, which resulted in the former borough of Londonderry becoming a policing district of the Royal Irish Constabulary. The Lord Lieutenant was also given power to add no more than forty-five constables to the already-established thirty to police the city.[1][2][3][4]

Belfast Town Police

Like many towns, Belfast had from its earliest days had a volunteer night watch, which in 1816 developed into a regular permanent day and night watch with a strength of around thirty.

The Belfast Police were originally armed with pikes and operated from a station in Rosemary Street, later Bridge Street, and finally operated out of the old town hall in Victoria Square.

From the 1830s the force was dressed and equipped along the lines of the London Metropolitan Police, wearing blue tail coats and reinforced 'stove-pipe' hats. The duties of the force encompassed not only maintaining law and order and preventing crime, but a range of civil duties such as removing graffiti, cleaning pavements, and fire-fighting.

Their jurisdiction encompassed the old town boundary on the Antrim side of the River Lagan and the Chief Constable was responsible to a Police Committee of the town council.

Belfast grew massively in size during the first half of the nineteenth century when workers flocked to the new industries, such as linen and shipbuilding. As the working-class population of the town grew this led to sectarian tension along 'flashpoint' areas where Protestant and Catholic areas met, which often erupted into rioting; especially during the Ulster 'marching season'.

From the 1850s onwards Belfast experienced serious communal rioting in 1857 and 1864, which the small town force of 165 men were unable to cope with due to their size, lack of training, and the noted partiality of many members of the force to take the side of the Protestant mob. To help quell such riots the help of the Irish Constabulary as an armed force was often called upon and, following a Royal Commission into the riots of 1864, legislation was passed to remove policing powers from the Borough of Belfast. The Belfast Police as a force was disbanded in 1865 and the task of policing taken over by the Irish Constabulary.

[1] http://america.pink/londonderry-borough-police_2742535.html – accessed 25 April 2016
[2] *Derry Beyond the Walls: Social and Economic Aspects of the Growth of Derry 1825-1850*. John Hume, 2002 (Ulster Historical Foundation)
[3] *RUC Historical Society Proceedings Summer/90*
[4] Londonderry Corporation minutes books – http://www.proni.gov.uk/index/search_the_archives/corporationarchive-3.htm

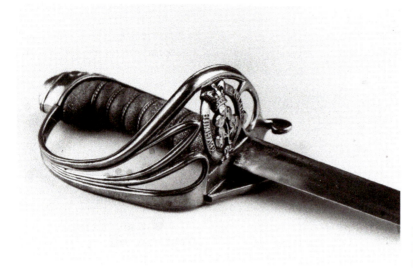

Irish Revenue
Police sword
c. 1850.

Irish Revenue Police

Illicit distillation, or poteen-making, has long been a clandestine activity in many parts of Ireland; however, it reached endemic levels in the early nineteenth century due to changes in the licensing laws. After several attempts by government to combat the practise by using the military and private contractors, an organised revenue police was established in 1836.

The force was 1,100 strong and was trained in the light infantry skills of the British army enabling its men to operate in small groups under their own initiative.

It was organised into four divisions with the bulk of the force being stationed along the west coast where the remoteness and many islands ensured good protection for any poteen-makers.

It normally carried out patrols in small groups under a lieutenant holding an excise commission and proved highly successful in pushing poteen-making on to islands off the west coast.

By the 1850s, the success of the force and changes in social attitudes towards alcohol promoted by the church – such as temperance and pioneer movements – led to questions over the need for such a specialised force.

In light of this, the Irish Revenue Police was disbanded in October 1857 and its duties and many of its men were taken over by the Irish Constabulary.

The Dublin Metropolitan Police

The Dublin Metropolitan Police was established by Act of Parliament in 1836 to replace the earlier ineffectual parish watch system and was modelled on the new London Metropolitan Police.

Although financed by Dublin City rates, unlike other UK city police forces then being established, in which control of the police lay with locally appointed police or watch committees, control of the DMP ultimately rested with the British authorities in Dublin Castle. For policing purposes the city was dived in to seven districts, lettered 'A' to 'G'.

A training depot was established at Kevin Street in Dublin and the regulations adopted were similar to that of the London force. It was an unarmed civil force and impartiality was imposed by a ban on any political expressions or activity. DMP members were also forbidden to enter public houses, except in the line of duty.

Recruits tended to come from neighbouring counties and the force was noted for the exceptional tallness of many of its members; one of whom, nicknamed 'Tiny', famously stood 7 foot 3 inches tall. This impression was accentuated by the issue of tall helmets of the English police pattern.

The rise of Irish trade unionism in the early 1900s led to the force being drawn into policing agitation and riots, most famously the Dublin general 'lock-out' of 1913 when the force was vilified in many quarters for its heavy-handed actions against striking workers.

The DMP's 'G' Division comprised a highly skilled detective branch that, due its effectiveness, was targeted by the IRA after the outbreak of the Irish War of Independence, during which many of its detectives were murdered.

As a civil force the DMP continued to operate into the new Irish Free State until it was amalgamated into the *Garda Síochána* in 1925.

DMP party with RIC Constable on parade for the official visit of King George V to Dublin, 1911.

DMP Constable on duty on O'Connell Street *c*. 1910.
Note the duty armband worn and the Nelson Pillar in the background.

Belfast Harbour Police

The Belfast Harbour Police (BHP) is the oldest police force in Ireland and one of the oldest in the UK, being established in 1824. Its responsibility was, and is, the protection of life and property and maintaining law and order in the harbour area of Belfast. The legal authority of the force was within the provisions of the Harbours, Docks and Piers Clauses Act of 1847, under which officers were attested.

The initial force was only one man strong, but grew to six in 1840 and sixty-five by the turn of the twentieth century. Due to disturbances and attacks in Belfast in the 1920s, officers were armed for the first time and it remains an armed police service to this day.

For the duration of the Second World War, the force was amalgamated with the RUC as part of Belfast 'H' District, with its chief officer in charge being given the rank of 1st Class District Inspector. The increased activity of the harbour and related industries during this period saw the strength of the force rise to a maximum of approximately 300.

The Harbour Police acquired their first motor boat – equipped with radio – in 1958, which enabled patrolling in previously hard-to-reach areas. The increase in the size and activity of the port combined with the onset of civil disorder in the Northern Ireland 'Troubles' saw the force reach a strength of 115 in 1969.

The introduction of new types of freight handling and civilianisation led from the 1980s to a decrease in the number of officers, although the main category of crime has always remained theft.

In December 2015 the BHP comprised of thirty-two officers and five civilian support staff.

The BHP today polices an area equal to a fifth of the size of the City of Belfast and focuses on community safety, crime prevention and detection, and road safety.

Members of the UHG (Belfast) River Patrol clearly showing the BHP blue peaked forage cap worn with khaki battledress. (Belfast Harbour Police)

BHP badges. Sergeants and Officers wore the officers' pattern badge to the left whilst constables wore the badge to the right.

Authors' Biographies

Hugh Forrester:
Hugh Forrester has been Curator of the Police Museum in Belfast since 1997 and is Honorary Secretary of the Police Historical Society (N.I.). He studied history at the University of Edinburgh and Archive Administration at the University of Liverpool. He has worked both as an archivist and museum curator throughout the UK; most recently as Director of The Somme Heritage Centre in Newtownards and as Curator of The Royal Inniskilling Fusiliers Museum in Enniskillen. In his current post he has been involved with the 'Healing Through Remembering' project, examining ways to deal with the memory and experience of the Northern Ireland 'Troubles', and edits *Proceedings*, the journal of the Police Historical Society (N.I.). His other interests include military history and vintage motorcycles. He is married and lives in Belfast and Enniskillen.

David R. Orr:
David R. Orr devotes much of his spare time to the field of military research and has supplied research material and photographs for several books. A Trustee of the Police Historical Society (N.I.), a member of the Society of Friends of the Airborne Museum, Oosterbeek, Society of Friends, Royal Irish Fusiliers Museum, The Police History Society and The Military History Society of Ireland, he has delivered talks to local history groups, historical societies, museums, and Regimental Associations. He is the author of *Duty Without Glory: The story of Ulster's Home Guard in the Second World War and the Cold War* and *RUC Spearhead: The Royal Ulster Constabulary Reserve Force 1950-1970*. He is also co-author of *The Rifles are There: 1st & 2nd Battalions, The Royal Ulster Rifles in the Second World War, A New Battlefield: The Royal Ulster Rifles in Korea 1950-51, Ulster Will Fight – Volume 1: Home Rule and the Ulster Volunteer Force 1886-1922*, and *Ulster Will Fight. Volume 2: The 36th (Ulster) Division in training and at war 1914-1918*. His family has served in the Royal Irish Constabulary, Ulster Special Constabulary, Royal Ulster Constabulary, and the Police Service of Northern Ireland. He is married with two sons and lives in Belfast.